Never Lose at Forex Again:
The Ultimate Risk Management Guide

Imane Al Omari

Copyright © 2024 Imane Al Omari

All rights reserved.

ISBN: 979-8-3218-5335-1

CONTENTS

	Acknowledgments	i
1	What Exactly Is Risk Management?	Pg 1
2	Minimum Capital Required for Forex	Pg 3
3	Concepts Of Drawdown and Maximum Drawdown	Pg 5
4	Don't Ever Gamble More Than 2% Of Your Trading Funds on A Single Trade	Pg 7
5	Risk to Reward Ratio	Pg 10
6	Study Your Losses to Realize Gains	Pg 12
7	Summary: Risk Management	Pg 14

ACKNOWLEDGMENTS

Writing this book wasn't a solitary journey. It involved countless battles with writer's block, exhilarating breakthroughs, and the unwavering support of some amazing people.

My Forex Familia

First and foremost, a massive thank you to the forex trading community. You guys rock! The shared knowledge, strategies, and (let's be honest) occasional war stories have been instrumental in shaping my understanding of risk management.

This Book Belongs to You Too

Finally, to every reader who picks up this book, thank you. Your desire to master risk management is what truly makes this book a success.

1 WHAT EXACTLY IS RISK MANAGEMENT?

One of the most important things to learn in trading is **how to handle risk**, which means dealing with the possibility of losing money. To do that, we need to understand and control the risks involved.

Many traders forget to look after their money properly and don't make a good plan. Instead, they just decide how much they're willing to lose in one trade and don't think it through carefully.
This approach is like gambling because it's based more on luck than strategy. It's essential to **manage risk** properly in trading to avoid gambling with your money.

Trading without rules to **manage risk** is just like gambling. Instead of thinking about **making money** in the long run, you're chasing big wins, like hitting a jackpot.

Having rules for **risk management** isn't just about protecting your money; *it can help you make more money over time.* To understand this, think about casinos in Las Vegas. People go there to win big, and some do, but the reason casinos always make money is because they make more from people who don't win. It's like the saying, **"The house holds the winning cards "**.

In trading, if you use **proper risk management** rules, you're more like the casino, increasing your chances of making money over time, rather than relying on luck like a gambler.

If you learn how to control your losses, you will have a chance of being profitable.

Forex trading is a bit like a math puzzle. You want everything to be on your side. Imagine it as a casino: the house usually has a 5% advantage over players. That small 5% is what can decide if you win or lose.

So, you want to be like a smart mathematician, not a reckless gambler. Why? Because in the long run, you want to be the one who comes out on top.

2 MINIMUM CAPITAL REQUIRED FOR FOREX

To start forex trading, you need money, but how much depends on your approach.

- **Education:** If you want formal classes or a mentor, it can cost hundreds to thousands of dollars. Alternatively, free online resources are available, but you need discipline and focus.

- **Tools:** Charting software can cost around $100 per month, while instant news feeds can range from hundreds to thousands of dollars monthly. Your broker may provide some for free.
    - *As an example, you can make use of the **TradingView** website, and it's also available as a downloadable app for your phone, featuring a free plan.*

- **Trading Capital:** You can open an account for as little as $25, but it's not recommended. To withstand losses and trade properly, starting with $5k to $10k is more realistic. Undercapitalization is a common reason for failure in forex trading.
    - *You can consider acquiring a funding account, but it's crucial to practice extensively on your demo account and implement effective risk management strategies before doing so. Failing to do this could result in losing your funding account in a very short time.*
    - *Example of a funding account is **MyForexFund** website.*

In essence, you need enough capital for trading and, if desired, education and tools, but it's crucial to be well-prepared and patient to increase your chances of success

3 CONCEPTS OF DRAWDOWN AND MAXIMUM DRAWDOWN

We've talked about how **risk management** can help you make money over time. But now, let's see what could happen if you don't use **risk management** rules.

Imagine you have $100,000, and you lose $50,000. How much of your money did you lose? It's 50%.

This is what traders call a **drawdown**. A **drawdown** is when your account goes down after a bunch of losing trades. *It's usually calculated by finding the difference between the highest amount of money you had and the lowest amount of money you had.* Traders usually talk about this as a percentage of their total account.

Period of Consecutive Losses

In trading, we're always searching for an advantage, which is why traders create systems. Having a trading system that's 70% profitable might sound great, but does it mean you'll win 7 out of every 10 trades?

Not necessarily! You can't predict which 70 out of 100 trades will be winners. You could even lose the first 30 trades and then win the next 70.

So, imagine losing 30 times in a row. Would you still be in the game? This is why risk management is crucial. Regardless of your trading system, you'll face losing streaks.

Even professional poker players, who earn their living from poker, experience rough patches. They manage risk by only risking a small part of their money so they can survive losing streaks.

AS A TRADER, YOU SHOULD DO THE SAME TO PROTECT YOUR CAPITAL.

Losses are a Normal Part of Trading

To be a successful forex trader, you need a trading plan that helps you endure tough times when you face big losses. **Part of this plan includes having rules for managing risks.**

One important rule is to only risk a small portion of your trading funds. This way, you can survive through losing streaks.

Keep in mind that if you follow these **money management rules** closely, you'll be more like the casino, and over time, you'll consistently come out on top.

4 DON'T EVER GAMBLE MORE THAN 2% OF YOUR TRADING FUNDS ON A SINGLE TRADE

Aiming to **keep your risk at 2% per trade** is a good idea, <u>but it might still be too much, especially if you're new to forex trading</u>. Let's look at an example to see why it's important to risk a small percentage of your capital compared to a higher percentage.

Here's an example to illustrate the importance of risking a small percentage of your capital:

Let's say you have $10,000 in your trading account.

Example	Risk Percentage	Risk Amount per Trade	Remaining Account Balance After One Losing Trade
Example1 (2%)	2%	$200	**$9,800**
Example2 (10%)	10%	$1,000	**$9,000**

The difference is clear: **by risking only 2% per trade**, you have a better chance of preserving your capital and surviving losing streaks. This is why many traders advocate for conservative **risk management** to protect their trading accounts.

Steps you should take to return to a point where you haven't gained or lost in trading?"

Imagine you started with $1,000 for trading, but due to some losses, your account balance is now down to $800. To get back to **breakeven** (which means having $1,000 again), you would need to:

- **Recognize the Loss:** Realize that you're currently $200 short of your initial $1,000.

- **Plan Carefully:** Create a plan for your trades. Decide that you'll risk no more than $20 (2% of $1,000) on each trade to prevent further losses.

- **Trade Cautiously:** Begin with smaller trade sizes, say, risking $20 per trade, to reduce the risk of losing more money.

- **Analyze and Learn:** Review your previous trades to understand what went wrong. Adjust your strategy to make better decisions.

- **Set Achievable Goals:** Don't expect to recover the entire $200 loss quickly. Aim for gradual progress and set smaller targets along the way.

- **Stay Disciplined:** Stick to your plan, use stop-loss orders, and avoid making impulsive trades driven by emotions.

- **Diversify:** Don't put all your money into one trade. Spread your risk by trading different assets.

- **Keep Learning:** Continue to improve your trading skills through education and practice.

- **Control Emotions:** Don't let your feelings guide your trades. Stay focused and make decisions based on your strategy.

- **Be Patient:** Understand that it might take some time to get back to breakeven. Consistent and careful trading is the key to success.

By following these steps, you can work toward getting your account balance back to where you started and then work on growing it further.

Outcome of your Trade

Use **"Gain & Loss Percentage Calculator"** to figure out how much you've gained or lost in your account.

It also tells you the percentage of your current balance needed to break even.

Remember, it's vital to risk only a small part of your account in each trade. This way, you can handle losing streaks and avoid big losses in your account.

5 RISK TO REWARD RATIO

To boost your chances of making money, you should trade in a way that lets you potentially earn three times more than you might lose.

When you use a **1:3 risk-to-reward ratio**, you increase your likelihood of being profitable in the long term.

Here's an example:

Trade	*Risk*	*Reward*	*Risk-to-Reward Ratio*
Trade 1	$100	$300	*1:3*
Trade 2	$50	$150	*1:3*
Trade 3	$80	$240	*1:3*
Trade 4	$120	$360	*1:3*

In this example, for each trade, you're risking a certain amount of money (**Risk**) with the potential to earn three times that amount (**Reward**). This is represented by a **1:3 risk-to-reward ratio**. It means that, on average, your potential gain is three times greater than your potential loss, which can enhance your profitability over time.

A good risk-to-reward ratio improves your chances of profiting in trading, even if you don't win every time.

However, it's not that simple. In real trades, setting a high **risk-to-reward ratio** can be challenging. For example, if you're a scalper and want to risk just

3 pips, aiming for a **1:3 ratio** means you need to gain 9 pips, considering the spread your broker charges.

You can adjust by reducing your trade size and widening your stop. For instance, if you're okay with risking 50 pips, you'd aim to gain 153 pips, which aligns better with a 3:1 ratio.

Remember, **risk-to-reward ratios aren't fixed**. They depend on factors like your *trading style, market conditions, and entry/exit points*. Long-term traders might seek a 10:1 ratio, while scalpers might accept as low as 0.7:1.

6 STUDY YOUR LOSSES TO REALIZE GAINS

Traders often focus on their winning trades and overlook their losing ones. However, there's valuable learning in those losses. Here are three ways to gain insights from unsuccessful trades.

Calculate your Performance!
To learn from your trading history, gather your past trade data. Calculate your:

- **Average Gain = Total Gain / Number of Profitable Trades.**

- **Average Loss = Total Loss / number of Unprofitable Trades.**

These numbers can be expressed as a **Profit/Loss Ratio**, which tells you the size of your **average profit** compared to your **average loss per trade**.

For instance, if your **Profit/Loss Ratio** is 0.67, it means your **average profit** is only 67% of your **average loss**. *This indicates that you've lost more money than you've gained.*

Additionally, your **Winning Percentage (number of profitable trades divided by total trades)** provides insights into your trading success. Analyzing these figures helps you identify weaknesses and improve your trading habits, such as sticking to your trade plans and making timely exits from both profitable and unprofitable trades.

Focus on Analyzing your Losing Trades in Depth!
To learn from your past mistakes, focus on your average losses because you have more control over them.

Even when you do your research, a trade can turn against you suddenly, changing a profitable trade into a losing one. It's how you handle these situations that matters for your success.

If you've faced such situations before, think about why you let a trade go bad for so long. Concentrating on your average losses can help you spot bad habits in your trading. You might be holding onto losing trades for too long. Try exiting them sooner before they reach your typical loss. This change can lead to better results.

You can be wrong more often than you're right and still do well. However, your average gains should be much larger than your average losses. You can measure this by calculating your trade expectancy.

Calculate your Trade Expectancy.
Expectancy is a way to figure out how much money you might make or lose on average for each trade based on your past performance.

It considers two things:
- The percentage of trades you won and how much you made on average from them.

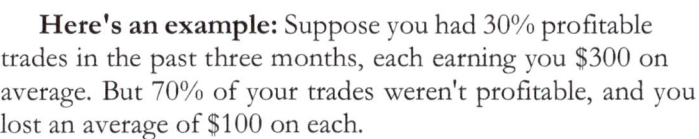

- The percentage of trades you lost and how much you lost on average.

Here's an example: Suppose you had 30% profitable trades in the past three months, each earning you $300 on average. But 70% of your trades weren't profitable, and you lost an average of $100 on each.
- By calculating **expectancy**, you can expect to gain about $20 for each trade:
  - **Expectancy** = (30% x $300) - (70% x $100)
  - **Expectancy** = ($90) - ($70) = $20

So, **expectancy** tells you how much you might win or lose, on average, in each trade.

The goal is to have a **<u>positive expectancy</u>**, meaning you make more on average than you lose. If it's not happening, review your losing trades to see where things are going wrong.

IT'S ESSENTIAL TO REMEMBER THAT YOUR TRADING SUCCESS RELIES HEAVILY ON YOUR EXPECTANCY.

7 SUMMARY: RISK MANAGEMENT

To start trading, you need some money, but how much depends on your trading approach. It's different for everyone.

Expect losses; they're part of trading. The more you lose, the harder it is to recover, which is why protecting your account is crucial.

Remember, it's essential to risk only a small part of your account in each trade. This way, you can handle losing streaks and prevent a significant account decline.

Big losses can quickly wipe out your account, so trade with a small percentage of your account. Less is often better in trading.

ABOUT THE AUTHOR

My ambition to take charge of my financial destiny and a deep-seated interest about the markets led me to start trading forex. After endless hours of research and independent study, I realized how important risk management is to long-term success.

The result of that trip is this guide, which is my opportunity to share to you, the aspiring trader, the knowledge, and tactics I've learned. Here, I stress how critical it is to have a thorough understanding of risk management. It's essential for creating a long-lasting trading career and generating future gains, not only about reducing losses.

Are you prepared to get off on your own trading journey? Together, let's control the markets!

www.ingramcontent.com/pod-product-compliance
Lightning Source LLC
Chambersburg PA
CBHW041946240526
45473CB00033B/622